Keith Worthington has re
taught mainly junior high s
the Calgary Board of Educa

Renate Worthington is a charter member of the Bow Valley Calligraphy Guild, and has participated in its projects, exhibitions, and publications for the past twenty-six years. Since her first course in 1979, she has studied with more than thirty instructors, and has shared her knowledge with her own calligraphy classes. Renate's commissions include work for schools, businesses, wedding planners, and individual clients. Working with Keith's poetry provides her with another opportunity to use images, moods, and letterforms suggested by words.

Keith and Renate have two daughters.

Puffs of Breath

poems by Keith Worthington
calligraphy by Renate Worthington

LA

LANGUAGE ART STUDIO

Library and Archives Canada Cataloguing in Publication

Worthington, Keith, 1950-
    Puffs of Breath: poems/by Keith Worthington; calligraphy by Renate Worthington.

ISBN/EAN 978-0-9784215-0-2 (pbk.)

    I. Worthington, Renate, 1947- II. Title

PS8645.O77P84 2007   C811'.6   C2007-905008-5

Printed in Canada by

for our family and friends

Thank you for supporting our art.
Keith Worthington
Renate Worthington

Acknowledgements

Thank you to Jim Kelly, my high school English teacher at Crescent Heights, the first person who treated me like a writer and therefore made me feel like a writer.

I am grateful to many of my own students, through the years, whose talents, enthusiasm, and perseverance motivated me to keep writing, to keep trying.

And to Renate who enhances my poetry and my life.

KW

CONTENTS

Breathing Outdoors

Breathing Together

Breathing in School

Breathing in the Dark

Just Breathing

Breathing Outdoors

A Bird Unseen

Gray puffs of breath
were all I could see
of a bird at work
in our Mayday tree.

The trunk concealed him
from my sight,
but I sensed him there
in the morning light.

He was after the seeds
in our wooden feeder
bits of energy
for a day of winter.

The food box swayed
from side to side,
his miniature movements
creating a tide.

Seeds were flying
in the frigid air,
littering the snow
and places bare.

I walked away
from this singular scene,
not needing to view
what I know had been.

Puffs of breath
in a wintery yard,
a gentle sight
for the human heart.

Delivery

Dressed in snowsuits
Jimmy and Ronald and I were bakers
who made the best snow loaves
and the best snow cakes
and the best snow cookies
in the whole world

Moulded by our mittened hands
they were all piping cold
and brilliant white

We loaded them on our toboggans
then trudged through knee deep drifts
delivering them around my backyard
to all the smiling customers
we could imagine

When our work was done
we sat on the back steps
said nothing
just chewed morsels of dough
that clung to our woolly hands

A Kid on the Rink

The only other person on the outdoor rink
is a kid about fifteen,
thick hair sticking out from under his ball cap
like hay from a loft.

He's practicing close in chances
where you need to roof it
before the goalie can recover
or before you get knocked on your ass.

I'm standing at centre ice
leaning on my stick Ken Dryden style
watching him.

A left-handed shot like me,
he drags the puck way back on his forehand
and then pulling it close to his left heel
flicks it upstairs into the twine.

Inside that ball cap
I bet he's imagining a goalmouth scramble
where the puck pops out
between a bunch of sticks and skates and shin pads—
a gift.
You can't practice too much to be ready for a moment like that.

What else motivates him to be out here by himself
three days after Christmas
just shooting the puck around
occasionally bursting down the wing
slapping a high one
the puck suddenly caught by the net like a doomed salmon?

And
what am I doing here
forty years after being fifteen
(and every year since)?

I went to the rink then, as I do now,
in search of solace
and finding it in the harsh familiarity of sharpened steel on hard ice
in the clearly defined boundaries of this world:
the boards, the rounded corners
the lines and circles
the stoic nets at each end.

Here was an escape from adult expectations
that were piling higher and colder
than snow scrapings from a fleet of Zambonis,
an escape from relationships
that never got to the heart of the matter—
Where was she while I skated?

Today, I choose not to talk to him,
preferring to imagine he is like me at fifteen:
shy, moody, glad to be alone.

THE CLEARLY DEFINED BOUNDARIES OF THIS WORLD

THE BOARDS
THE ROUNDED CORNERS
THE LINES AND CIRCLES
THE STOIC NETS AT EACH END

Neighbourhood Rink

I am drawn
even now, decades later,
to our neighbourhood rink
    where on this wintery Saturday morning
    memories return without warning.

At just such a place
I skated for the first time
and in a forgotten shinny game
scored my first goal
    became inspired
    played until I was so tired.

On those glorious days
of ice and snow and sun
for a few hours
the friends of childhood became rivals.
We shouted,
    "Second captain, first pick!"
    (Tighten your skates and grab your stick.)

Hab sweaters and Leaf sweaters
a Bruin, Blackhawk, Red Wing or Ranger—
Worshippers of the Original Six,
we battled against each other.
"I'm The Rocket!"
"I'm The Big M!"
We were free to imagine
    to skate, to score
    maybe a hat trick, maybe more.

Later in the skate shack,
we rested up and warmed up
    agonizing over frozen toes—
    a pop and a chocolate bar to go.

This morning,
the boarded rink is a frozen ghost town.
    The ice awaits; it's ready for fun
    but nowadays the children do not come.

Late March

Crocuses huddle together,
their puckered, mauve heads
staring down at the pale grass
until the spring sun
warms their furry shoulders

Early April

I can feel the sun grow stronger
I can see the evening's longer

My world is warming day by day
Growth and greenery on their way

There are countless sun ray reasons
To celebrate this change of seasons

I can feel the sun
grow stronger
I can see
the evening's longer
my world is warming
day by day

THERE ARE
COUNTLESS
SUNRAY
REASONS
TO CELEBRATE
THIS CHANGE
OF SEASONS

growth and
greenery
on their way

Spring Training Game

Gulls, like under-sized ball players,
stroll the local community diamond
in their nearly identical white and gray uniforms.

Even with the April sun shining down
(the most glorious stadium light in the solar system),
no names or numbers are visible
so I can't tell who is who.

I am left to wonder:
Are they the home team
or the visitors who just flew into town?

Meadow Tree

I smile when I see you again,
grateful that you are still here—
still standing
at the edge of the meadow.

You've changed.
Now one lower branch is
bent, drooping, touching ground,
and the dry winds of a harder winter
have reddened many of your needles.

Yet, no matter what has happened in your life,
no matter what insensitive forces have assailed you,
you are still you.

And me?
I am still me
despite my harder winter,
despite my own harsh encounters.

That's why I count you as a friend.
Another year has passed
but we accept each other:
        for what we were
        for what we are
        for what we will become.

Etherington Creek

Creek, like me, you tumble and fall
and you can't be sure
what's around the next bend.

Rocks and logs and weeds
might slow you down
but you find ways
to continue your journey,
and while creatures explore your edges,
your darkest depths are for more private eyes.

Let me come with you, creek;
we'll search together
for what it is that lies beyond
the current rush and babble
of our lives.

Creek, like me, you tumble and fall
And you can't be sure
              what's around the next bend

              Rocks and logs and weeds
                          might slow you down
                          But you find ways
                    To continue your journey
And while creatures explore your edges
              your darkest depths are for more private eyes

                    Let me come with you, creek,
                          we'll search together
              For what it is that lies beyond
        The current rush and babble
                          of our lives

West of Longview

A white-thatched mountain
stands at the end of the valley
and watches over our campsite
like a protective ancestor.

Trees are not welcome at his summit,
but gather on lower reaches
like obedient grandchildren.

Snow has spilled down his sides
and even now, in June,
clings stubbornly to wrinkled ledges.

I'm glad to know
he'll be here next year, if I return,
still calmly viewing less permanent lives.

Solstice
(thinking of Marion)

This afternoon several peonies
hang like the moons of Jupiter
against the backdrop of my dark green hedge.

They declare, "We're back!
In December, you never gave us a thought.
Now it is glorious June,
our time to deliver flowery gifts.
Remember us,
for we and the sun will not reach
this northern apex again."

The Gift

With our all-weather friends
we strolled Marl Lake loop
a summertime gang
a carefree troupe.

Though Christmas was far
from our July-camp minds
a purple clematis
made us think of that time.

It had climbed a spruce
a Charlie Brown tree
close by the trail
for all to see.

It wound to the top
like a string full of lights
where a star-burst flower
made the forest bright.

It was like a gift
for a distant Yuletide
a Christmas greeting
from the warmth of July.

It wound to the top like a string full of lights.

Combination

Green on blue
trees against sky
westerly winds
and a hawk's faint cry

Green on blue
hills to the west
marking a place
where your mind can rest

Green on blue
Alberta in July
summer in bloom
the grasses grow high

Green on blue
enjoy it while you can
closer to nature
closer to this land

Fate of a Lodge Pole Pine

You cling to that ledge
like a starving madman.

Don't you know
there are better places to grow?

When you were young
solid earth nourished you
and held your roots in place.

Now
that earth is abandoning you
slipping away month by month
like an unfaithful lover.

You are doomed to a death
before your time
but still you reach
for the sun and heavens beyond.

I wish that you had known
there are better places you might have grown.

Kananaskis Country

Carry on without me
when I've gone back to the city.

Be here at the edge of the Rockies:
bloom and grow
move and blow
shine, rain, live on.
Be a companion
to others who come down the trail.

Carry on without me
when I've gone.

So as I wait at a stoplight in rush hour traffic,
I can smell the delicate sweetness of your wild meadow flowers.

And after I turn off my television set,
I can see your mountains brushing away
the slate gray clouds of a summer storm.

And late at night, as I lie awake in my civilized bedroom,
 I can hear untarnished wind through dark pine branches.

Carry on without me,
so I know in my heart that this place continues to be.

KANANASKIS COUNTRY

Carry on without me
    when I've gone

Be here at the edge of the Rockies
Bloom and grow
Move and blow
Shine, rain, live on
Be a companion
    to others who come down the trail to this place

Carry on without me
    when I've gone back to the city

So as I wait at a stoplight in rush hour traffic
I can smell the incredibly delicate sweetness
    of your wild meadow flowers
And after I turn off my television set
I see your mountains brushing away the slate gray clouds
    of a summer storm
And late at night, as I lie awake in my civilized bedroom
I can hear the movement of untarnished wind
    through your dark pine branches

Carry on without me
So I know in my heart that this place continues to be

Watching Summer Rain

During the calm of a dark green evening
there is something to respect
about a summer rain that comes
straight down
forthright like a friend.

down
down
no gust of wind
no meanness
just down
down

then eases back

a moment later
down again
no anger here

It leaves behind
a dripping, gurgling world
in which it is easier to breathe.

DURING THE CALM OF A DARK GREEN EVENING
THERE IS SOMETHING TO RESPECT
ABOUT A SUMMER RAIN THAT COMES
STRAIGHT DOWN
FORTHRIGHT LIKE A FRIEND
DOWN
DOWN
NO GUST OF WIND
NO MEANNESS
JUST DOWN
DOWN
THEN EASES BACK
A MOMENT LATER
DOWN
AGAIN
NO ANGER HERE
IT LEAVES BEHIND
A DRIPPING GURGLING WORLD
IN WHICH IT IS EASIER TO BREATHE

Alberta Forecast

One fine morning in July
(I'm sorry I cannot specify)
Puffs of cloud will saunter by
Through a wide, untroubled sky

Try to savor it while you may
This could be the very best day
To paint the barn or cut the hay
Or find a stream and drift away

First Teeing Ground

Here in this privileged sanctuary
as green as the Sherwood Forest of our childhoods,
the most important consideration in this world
is our first drive of the morning.

It is planned, rehearsed, and executed
in the quietness of the moment.
We relish this fresh start:
another chance, sometime today, to make a magical shot:
the ball rolling delightfully close to the hole
or, be still our hearts, into the hole.

But first, to feel that solid contact—
club against ball
and then to watch it soar
ball against sky
unaffected by spin or wind
arcing toward a pleasing destination
seen in our mind's eye just moments before.

Then it connects with turf,
a powerful bounce straight ahead,
another—softer, and another, softer yet.
After that, it settles into a roll, eases to a stop—
white sphere against green grass.
       So far.
       So good.

Drive

Westward to the mountains
I'm cruising on Highway One
Turning down the visor
Against the melting sun

I recognize a feeling
Deep within my soul
Prairie spaces comfort me
So does the open road

The sky is my companion
The fields are by my side
Here on Alberta's western shore
Wild grasses are the tide

My van feels like a sailing ship
Being tossed by restless dreams
Tacking through the foothills
Guided by evergreens

Spruce trees and lodge pole pines
Surviving as best they can
Here where the wind can blow so hard
They're trying to make a stand

Westward through the mountains
That hide the setting sun
Flipping up the visor
I'm staying on Highway One

wild grasses

Here on Alberta's western shore

wild grasses

wild grasses are the tide

Cabin Clothesline

Don't leave your swimsuit on the floor;
the clothesline stands outside the door.

It holds the artifacts from a day
we spent at the beach not far away.

So hang yours there with all the rest;
add to the shrine of sportswear's best.

You'll find a relic from everyone
drying there in the Shuswap sun:

> Garish towels point to the ground.
> (They may look loud, but don't make a sound.)
>
> Boxers, surf shorts and sleeveless tops
> hang as limp as overused mops.
>
> Stripes, solids, and even some plaid
> reflect the art of a sculptor gone mad.

So many possessions have come this way,
it's a jumble of colors late in the day.

Orange and blue, yellow and green
celebrate together this summertime scene.

STRIPES SOLIDS and even some PLAID REFLECT THE ART OF A SCULPTOR GONE MAD

Intruders

Who's that shuffling down my street?
Why it's just a gang of autumn leaves,

looking tough and walking the walk,
in a hurry and full of talk.

Here on August's hottest day,
if they stop, I'll have this to say:

"Vamoose! Move along! It's not your time.
October is far from my summer mind.

"Climb back in the towering trees;
turn yourselves back to green.

"Quit the street and its hardened ways;
save your strutting for colder days."

Who's that
shuffling
down the street?
Why, it's just
a gang of
autumn leaves
looking tough
and walking
the walk
in a hurry
and full of talk

Alberta Autumn

By late October, a cold north wind,
enemy to all that summer stood for,
invades the trees
and strips them nearly bare.

Hordes of yellow and brown leaves
scrape their dry, wrinkled bodies
as they flip and tumble madly
    down
       my
          deserted street.

I do not understand.

Why are they in such a hurry,
when their only destination can be
 Canadian winter?

By late October
a cold north wind
ENEMY TO ALL THAT SUMMER STOOD FOR
invades the trees
and strips
them NEARLY BARE
HORDES OF YELLOW AND BROWN LEAVES
SCRAPE THEIR DRY, WRINKLED BODIES
AS THEY FLIP AND TUMBLE MADLY
DOWN MY DESERTED STREET.
I do not understand.
Why are they in such a hurry
WHEN THEIR
ONLY DESTINATION
CAN BE
Canadian winter?

Early Snow

One good thing about an early snow,
it'll cover up a lot of mistakes
like elm tree leaves I neglected to rake.

And those backyard holes I meant to fill
that lie near that drooping spruce bough,
well, they look as though they're filled in now.

I always wish a surprising snow
could just as well cover up my fears,
ones that wake me when they steal so near.

A snowfall could bury them hour by hour,
maybe even freeze them to death,
my fears in a heap, out of breath.

But I know the ways of a November sun;
it still has strength to melt the snow,
so my leaves and fears are again exposed.

BUT I KNOW
THE WAYS
OF A
NOVEMBER SUN
IT STILL HAS
STRENGTH
TO MELT
THE SNOW
SO MY LEAVES
AND FEARS
ARE AGAIN
EXPOSED

November Memories

It wasn't fall; it wasn't winter;
it was November.
It wasn't warm; it wasn't pretty,
but I remember:

A dried-out, shriveled pumpkin
sat by the backyard door;
a frosty, golden maple leaf
melted on the kitchen floor.

A squirrel scurried across the yard;
time was running low;
it sensed that unforgiving winds
would soon begin to blow.

Old soldiers dressed in Legion blazers
stood reverently at attention;
their blood-red poppies symbolized
what hearts couldn't bear to mention.

Birds, on the wing, left this land
for warmer, easier climes,
while ragged ponies in frozen fields
endured the colder times.

The north wind rattled twigs and branches
as it cut through naked trees.
Were the rivers really slowing down
or was it just November in me?

NOVEMBER

WERE
THE
RIVERS
REALLY
SLOWING
DOWN
OR
WAS
IT
JUST
NOVEMBER
IN
ME?

Remembrance

November thirteenth,
I am walking across the schoolyard
staring at the soft pink Alberta sunrise,
and thinking, in fragments,
about the day ahead with my junior high students.

Almost underfoot, I see a Remembrance poppy,
scarlet against the faded yellow turf.

Suddenly, the schoolyard is a battlefield
and the poppy is a bloodstain on a forest floor,
and the scavenger gulls I meet daily
are puffs of artillery smoke.

I am afraid.
I have dropped my rifle
and my best buddy is at my feet, not moving.
The bloodstain is his: larger, darker now.
The noise seems from every direction,
whistling through and cracking against trees
that all look the same in fog and smoke.

I turn, looking for my mates,
and then—
a stunning impact against my left hip,
crushes my body to the ground.
Christ, I can't move my legs.
My upper body is twisted
and pressed against my friend,
his leaking blood mixing with my own.

This is not right;
this is not the way to finish.

As the battle rages on,
dark trees stand over us,
unmoved by the mayhem.

Consciousness fades.
In sleep I will make my escape,
      an angel to carry me
      an angel to carry me
army green against her soft whiteness.

Safely in her arms, I smell her sweet scent.
I am hers.

Here and now—
in front of me is an orange metal door,
a back entrance to my school.
I open it, stepping into boiler-warmed air
and silence.
I am alone in this familiar hallway,
checkerboard linoleum beneath my feet.

But I remember.

Winter's Time

Like a bird of prey,
gray winter hangs above
the frozen foothills west of Calgary,
then silently descends upon the city,
its icy talons gripping
buildings and trees and people.

LIKE A BIRD OF PREY
THE GRAY WINTER HANGS ABOVE
THE FROZEN FOOTHILLS WEST OF CALGARY
THEN SILENTLY DESCENDS UPON THE CITY
ITS ICY TALONS GRIPPING
BUILDINGS AND TREES AND PEOPLE.

K. WORTHINGTON

Deep Snow

A billion crystals cling together
Through December's whitening weather
In this frozen northern sphere
Far from the sun at this time of year
Deep snow, deep Christmas, deep snow

Under the mounds and through the drifts
Imagine all the hidden gifts
Find the memories buried beneath
Recall the warmth of the Yuletide feast
Deep snow, deep Christmas, deep snow

Hear the wind in the white-coated trees
Let her stories put you at ease
And when the dark of evening comes
Immerse yourself in the ancient songs
Deep snow, deep Christmas, deep snow

Under the mounds
and through the drifts
Imagine all the hidden gifts
Find the memories buried beneath
Recall the warmth
of the Yuletide feast

deep snow

deep Christmas

deep snow

A Toast

What's to be said about Christmas
Unless it's spoken from the heart
Don't let other obligations
Keep us worlds apart

We'll sit beside our well-lit tree
It has such a wondrous glow
Silvery tinsel and shiny spheres
Remind us of long ago

We'll think of loved ones near and far
Some as far as eternity
We'll raise a glass to our storied past
And our current reality

Silvery tinsel
and shiny spheres
Remind us
of long ago

Breathing Together

Imagining Friar Park

I should like to have visited Friar Park
when George was there at home.
Through his gardens we would have strolled,
just he and I and his gnomes.

He might have taught me about his trees
and flowers he liked to grow.
He would have shown me lily ponds
and told of caves below.

I like to think there was a shed
with a rake, a spade, a hoe.
We would have spent a quiet time
tending beds and rows.

He might have looked me in the eye
and questioned the state of my heart.
Though we'd just met, he might have known
that I was in the dark.

I'm sure he would have reaffirmed
the Lord is here within
and when I shun my worldly ways
I'll be close to Him.

It would have been a pleasant time,
the hours drifting away.
A cup of tea by his fireplace
would have made a perfect day.

(Friar Park was the home of my hero, George Harrison, who
once was a Beatle but became a gardener.)

Quiet Love

Quiet love my father gave me;
quiet love it felt so good.
Quiet love my father gave me,
as every parent should.

Seldom in an open way,
rarely ever spoken,
a side by side kind of feeling,
no promise ever broken.

We used to share his big armchair,
a world of him and me.
That was all I ever needed
to make some days complete.

When I think of all the memories
during a time of calm reflection,
the years slide away like a gentle tide
to reveal my true affection.

Quiet love my father gave me;
quiet love has stayed right here.
The love my father gave me
is enough for all my years.

Quiet love
my father gave me
Quiet love
it felt so good

Lunch Pail Cookies

Lunch pail cookies were the best they could be
when my dad saved them just for me.

Our back porch light showed him the way,
home from the shops on dark winter days.

Up the snowy steps, he came in the door
as a gust of winter stole across the floor.

He handed me the pail, as he gave Mom a kiss;
I took it to the counter and undid the clips.

Like a black metal book, I folded it open;
our kitchen filled with love—no words spoken.

On one side was a Thermos, secure in its place;
on the other side, wax paper filled up the space.

My eager hands searched; I knew what I'd find,
lunch pail cookies—the peanut butter kind.

Peanut butter cookies—the best they could be,
a sweet sign of love my dad saved for me.

On one side was a Thermos,
secure in its place
On the other side, wax paper
filled up the space

Kitchen Cupboards

Looking through a sunlit haze of fifty years
I see Mom, much taller than me,
busy in her kitchen.
She reaches into white cupboards
above brown countertops.
She wears a yellow housedress
and with a smoothness of motion
that is only gained through daily routine,
she removes ingredients for baking.

On occasions when Mom is elsewhere,
in the basement beside her wringer washer
or on the back porch hauling in a clothesline bounty
of white sheets and work clothes,
I use a long-legged, wooden stool to climb up.

Then, like a mountaineer,
I lean out over the linoleum far below
and swing open a door as I duck beneath it.

The cupboard smells good right away,
an exotic conglomeration of tin containers
that can keep their ingredients
but not their smells contained:
cinnamon, clove, nutmeg, dry mustard.

When they are empty, Mom gives them to me
so I can re-fill them with my own riches:
lucky rocks, marbles, nickels, candy.

Nowadays, I cherish both memories,
those of the cupboard and those of the lady
who filled shelves with pungent treasures for her family.

Gratitude

We grew up on unpaved streets
lined with newly-built, post-war bungalows
that sat unpretentiously on half-acre lots.
And we played in back alleys filled with the wild greenery
of bushes, weeds, and unkempt trees.
   And now, we are burying our fathers.

In springtime, we threw baseballs that cracked windows
or chipped the brittle shingles off our homes.
We played marathon games of hide and seek
but slipped inside for an hour
to watch our brand new black and white televisions.

On Dominion Day, the adults raised the Red Ensign
and saluted a summer of freedom.
We sipped Orange Crush from brown-rippled bottles
and ran glorious foot races across the community grounds.
Later, we filled up on free hotdogs
but somehow left room for Dixie Cups
consumed with tongue-depressor wooden spoons.
We admired fin-tailed family cars
that cruised into our driveways and lives.
Sunday afternoons, we drove through the countryside
to Cochrane, for more ice cream.

On autumn Saturdays, at the park,
we threw footballs across the Alberta sky
and watched them bounce crazily
through a dried expanse of wind-blown leaves
or better yet, land softly in the outstretched hands
of blue-jeaned wide receivers.

In winter, we skated on outdoor rinks
that had been scraped clean, then flooded on late evenings-
frozen gifts for the neighborhood children.
After shinny, we warmed up in the skate shack
agonizing over frozen toes and fingers.
And is it too late to say thank you
for those precious seasons of our youth?
   Perhaps not, as we are burying our fathers.

Beaches, Stars, and Home

A little girl rides in the back of the car;
shining close by is the evening star.

Her dad's day of driving is bringing her home
across the prairies and close to the Bow.

She's a little bit lost in a summertime dream
as she thinks of her family and places they've been.

The beach beside Gimli is miles behind
but an image remains of that sun-drenched time.

Soon she is drifting as the fields roll by
and the sun is asleep below a darkening sky.

The kids near Mom are dreaming dreams too
but Dad—he drives on because that's what dads do.

By the time she awakes they've traveled so far
she sees Calgary is filled with streetlight stars.

They guide the car home, a turn to the right,
within a few moments the house is in sight.

It looks just the same and it feels good too;
it's the place she belongs when August is through.

For the beach is not home and home's not the beach;
these are the things that summer times teach.

FOR THE BEACH
IS NOT HOME
AND HOME'S
NOT THE BEACH
THESE ARE THE THINGS
THAT SUMMER
TIMES TEACH

Fathers and Daughters

When I see a kite against the sky
I think about you and me
and how we touch each other's lives
so very naturally.

But when a kite strains to set itself free
it needs a caring hand.
How can it know what freedom entails?
How can it understand?

Daughter, I know, you want to soar
you want your freedom too.
But I'll hold on for just awhile
and believe it's best for you.

Beautiful Women

Sometimes I imagine beautiful women asleep in their beds.
(I have airbrushed their men out of the picture.)
Each lady is wrapped in darkness, protected by silence
and ensconced in flannel pajamas or a t-shirt and boxers.

High heels have been kicked into crowded closets
and bras stuffed into hard to close drawers.
Weighty necklaces have been removed;
powders and pastes washed away.

These women are little girls again,
just so,
each one sleeping and perhaps dreaming of a dad
who softly enters the room
draws a cover over her exposed shoulder
and at the same time
bends to place a kiss on that familiar forehead.

Closing the door as he leaves,
he shuts out all the glaring requirements of her adult life.

First Kiss

I see you standing far across the room
at this crowded funeral reception.
Between us, the heads of mostly strangers
bob on a murmuring sea of dark suits and black dresses.
The unavoidable clinking of cups and saucers
adds to the ritual.
Our dead classmate reclines a few meters away,
no doubt as pale as the china,
an ear perhaps pressed against the satin lining.

How peculiar,
thirty years after my first kiss
and, I assume, your first kiss.
I wonder if the number of friends
and lovers and spouses
who have touched your lips with theirs
is as modest as the number who have touched mine.
My main memory of that day
is a thirteen year old's chase into the back alley,
then warmth, delicateness,
such a surprise.

I caught up with you behind your garage
both of us skidding on gravel.
Didn't know what to say.
Didn't know what to do.
Holding tight as a wrestler to my neighbour girl
heart pounding,
who's watching?
Nothing to do but kiss you.
Resistance at first,
laughter too.
Then with my lips against your teeth
you relaxed into it.
My world suddenly adrift
behind closed eyes
and the smell of Ivory soap.

I let go first,
suddenly afraid that you wouldn't.
Then I bolted for home
slamming fence gates behind me
heart racing still
not daring to look back
anxious for the safety of my room
and baseball and glove.

With great regret
I will resist the temptation
to walk sideways through these mourners
and remind you who I am.

Driving the Avenue

A sub-culture of young people swarms
    along the too-narrow sidewalks
Neon lights bathe them
    in pale pink and orange

Eat
    Drink
        and meet the love of your life
        in a smoky, noisy barroom
        where hockey game highlights
        and rock videos flash like bad dreams
        from overhead televisions

Me?
I'll just carefully drive by all of this
    my sixteen year old daughter
    in the passenger seat beside me
    not saying a word
    just looking intently

At a stop light
    young adults shuffle through a crosswalk
    in front of us
One of them
    taps gently on the hood of my car
    grins like a madman
    gives us an exaggerated wave
    turns away
    laughs with his friends
    and keeps walking
I furtively glance to see
    if the car door is locked
I look at Lisa; she is smiling

When the light changes
    I'll hurry her away from all this
    and take her home
        Safe
        Warm
        Comfortable home

A sub-culture of young people swarms
along the two-narrow sidewalks
NEON LIGHTS bathe them
in pale PINK AND ORANGE
EAT DRINK
and meet the love of your life
in a smoky, noisy barroom
where HOCKEY GAME highlights
and rock videos flash like bad dreams
from overhead televisions

Me?
I'll just carefully drive by
all of this
My sixteen year old daughter
in the passenger seat beside me
not saying a word
just looking intently

Hawaiian Sun

The same sun that sank as heavily as a warrior's shield
into the ocean last evening
has risen from behind an easterly mountain.

She now glides toward an afternoon apex
in her own cloudless, blue swimming pool
just above me in mine.

Yesterday, when she departed
leaving smears of tangerine against the sky
I experienced a momentary sense of loss and regret.

Yet today,
I have taken her re-appearance so matter of factly
that I never acknowledged her until this moment.

And you, my darling,
who sank last night beneath your covers
are again close by
reclining on your pool lounger
matter of factly
unacknowledged until this moment.

Go to Bed Early

We should go to bed early
But we'll stay up late
See how the time change
Affects our fate
Bring our own pillows
For a dream-like state
We'll go to bed early
But we'll stay up late

Imagine just the two of us
Adrift at sea
At every port-o-call
We can do as we please
Shop in the market
Where the duty's free
And drink white rum
'Neath the tropical trees

Maybe later on
We'll zoom to outer space
Have a rendezvous
In a starry place
A thousand suns will shine
On your beautiful face
And keep my hopes alive
For a state of grace

So we'll go to bed early
But we'll stay up late
See how the time change
Affects our fate
Bring our own pillows
For a dream-like state
Go to bed early
And stay up late

Poem Cloud

A poem cloud passed overhead;
I knew that you had signed it.
A thundershower was hanging near,
but I really didn't mind it.

An airy message of such delight,
I was hoping I might find it.
And best of all, I clearly saw
your silvery love had lined it.

And best of all
I clearly saw
your silvery love
had lined it.

Aching Through Every Bone

Maybe we call it falling in love
because it can be a downward spiral

You're a sky diver whose chute doesn't open
      just falling
           falling
                no control

You're not looking forward to the end either
      no happily ever after here
           trouble ahead
                splat

Except–
      you survive
      somehow you survive

My God, you get up
though you're aching through every bone

You walk out of that field
dusting yourself off, thinking
Geez, I hope no one saw that
      but someone did
maybe your best friend
and he asks, all concerned,
      "Are you okay?"
And you say,
      "Yeah, sure, I'm fine,"
but you're not

You're aching through every bone
and you just wanna go home

Good Intentions

This evening
my intention was to count the stars
one at a time
as they appeared in the summer sky.

I made a good start too
but then my eyes were drawn to you.

And when I looked above again
well, the task was overwhelming.
Where had I left off?
Which jewel was next to be counted?

Back to you—
No less daunting a task:
to count the number of times
you have been on my mind.

Above—
darkness—pierced in a billion places.

Perhaps tomorrow night.

If Only

When I tell you that I love you
do you think the less of me?
Do you shake your head, not understand
and wish I would let things be?

When I tell you that I have no choice,
I'm a victim of circumstance,
does it change your mind in any way
or just earn me a sidelong glance?

If only I were as strong as you
my heart in a different space,
where love is never mentioned
where love hides her shining face.

Into Dark Blue (Kananaskis Night Walk)

The moon stayed clear of invading clouds,
would not wear their confining shroud.
She revealed a side that made me proud
and of course I thought of you.

As I stumbled along my darkened way
the stars were drowning in a sea of gray,
the treetops nodded and began to sway,
as the wind was blowing through.

I tried to cast off this sense of dread;
the woods were as dark as Frost once said.
Into them I could be easily led;
they were lovely and deep it's true.

Dylan was right; I could be tangled within,
lose myself and forget my sins,
wait for the rain or sleet to begin,
but I had to keep looking for you.

My mind raced on like the clouds above.
Is there ever a choice in who we love?
Can I tame the hawk and protect the dove?
Is there nothing I can do?

The wild night took me to the brink;
I found myself at the abandoned rink,
a place that might give me room to think,
but who was kidding who?
I was just into dark blue.

How Dare You

How dare you wake me from a winter's nap
–the rude ringing of my telephone—
to tell me that you won't be coming after all
that you won't be coming again.
You've had enough.
It's all too difficult.
Goodbye.

The nap, you see, was much different.
Warm fingers from a benevolent sun
had reached over my book
gently pressed my eyes closed
and helped me escape from all considerations.

At that point, I imagined you were beside me
holding my hand in yours
guiding me toward an understanding
that would have required neither a nap
nor a phone call.

Away

On a station platform
in the rebellious rain
I stand alone
waiting
for a train that does not stop here.

Behind me
water cascades over the eaves
and slaps the wooden planks.

The train approaches.
Its yellow eye
brightens the steel rails
and shines accusingly on me.

I am here grasping at straws
imagining I may catch a glimpse of her
one more time.

From the warm light of a rain-soaked sleeping car
she will see me and...
look alarmed, feel regret, change her mind,
press her hands against the window—

It does not happen.

More quickly than I imagined
the train rumbles by.
The figures in the rain-distorted windows
are silhouettes.
I only feel her go by, ghost-like.

The rain persists, strengthens;
thunder and lightning bombard me.
The train calls,
"Away, away, away,"
as I watch the last coach
and her
glide out of my life.

Synchronicity

It is a winter poem
that should have been enjoyed months ago
but wasn't.
So one spring day
I read with my students
Robert Frost's "The Wood-pile".

And the very next day,
I'm telling you, the very next day
not two minutes from our city school
a wood-pile is erected.
It is the remains of a front yard spruce tree,
climbed and stripped and cut by hired hands.

Unlike Frost
I am not intrigued
by this neatly piled stack of wood,
though its creators are still there
busying themselves with the cleanup
of spruce boughs, dry needles, and pale sawdust.

But I am intrigued
by the way experiences align themselves
just beyond our understanding,
like approaching figures cloaked in fog:

> One day you hear the name of an acquaintance from years ago;
> the next, you see her at an entrance to an elevator.
>
> You think about an old friend for the first time in a long time;
> hours later, he calls.
>
> You're driving on your way to visit her,
> and *your* song comes on the radio.

The cylinders tumble so smoothly into place.

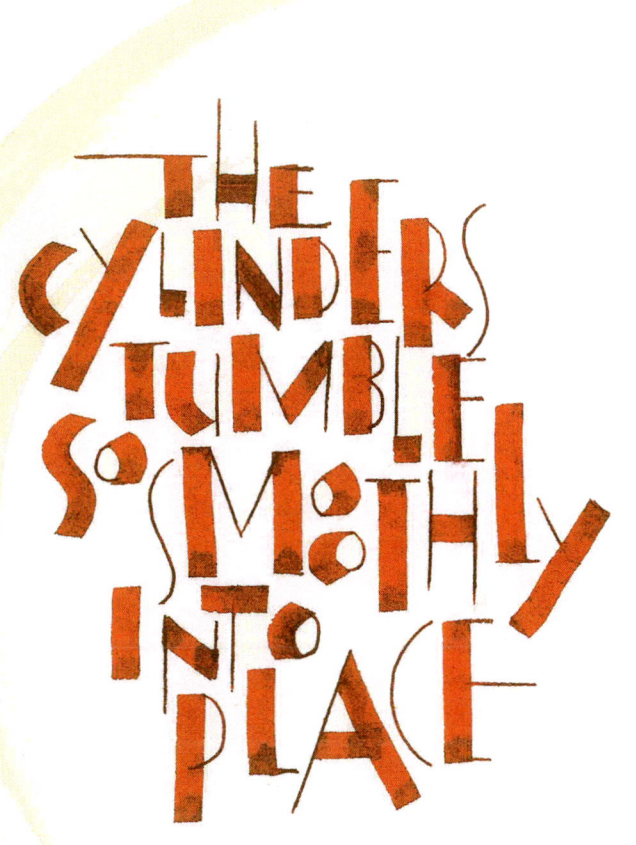

Not Broadway

I left the stage in a foul mood,
knew my actions would be misconstrued,
started my car, continued to brood,
my head and heart in a family feud.

I get so weary of this part I play,
a tired actor on a darkening stage.
I wonder if there's another way
to perform this tragic matinee.

Can't I be the hero of the story,
save us all, get the glory,
see the audience rise to its feet,
and hear applause from your front row seat?

Today I Imagine

Today I imagine that you have moved to a foreign land far away,
one of those exotic islands whose name or geographic location
I can never quite remember.

You are happy there: safe and secure.

Your once vivid memories of your life in Canada and my little part in it
have faded like an old summer t-shirt.

For you, island life is good in the eye-squinting sunshine
of a tropical beach community.

A new circle of friends has immersed you in a culture of ex-patriots:
barbeques on a sandy point and swims by moonlight.

Your face is tanned; your feet calloused.

Now, as I stroll out of Safeway,
plastic grocery bag handles cutting the circulation from my fingers,
I see your car searching for a parking space.

My heart sinks to the warm pavement and melts,
leaving a guava-pink stain.

A Song for You

I've got a song for you
It's one they call the blues
I've got a song for you
It's one they call the blues
I don't want it no more
So I'm givin' it to you

It gets me down
It drags me through the dirt
It gets me down
It drags me through the dirt
It's full of pain
It's full of truth and hurt

Someone gave it to me
But it's time I pass it on
Someone gave it to me
But it's time I pass it on
You're the next in line
Though you ain't done me wrong

You know you can't refuse
It's a cross you'll have to bear
Too bad you can't refuse
It's a cross you'll have to bear
There's no escaping it
The blues are everywhere

I've got a song for you
it's one they call
the Blues

About Your Leaving

The stars express no sympathy
toward your selfishness.
You'd like to think you could ignore
their distant callousness.

Coldly, they look down on you
from the wide Alberta sky.
They keep their distance from your woes
and you know the reasons why.

When daytime comes, the sun—she hides
behind her shield of gray,
stares like a Cyclops at your fate,
but never has a thing to say.

The river slows down to look at you,
then silently moves along.
It'll warn some others on its way
not to sing your lonely song.

The trees don't reach to comfort you,
they continue to be unmoved
by the excuses you make and the chances you take
and the way you play us all for fools.

Only the fields wave a gentle good-bye
and try to whisper to your soul,
as you walk toward a distant line
where your future will unfold.

ONLY THE FIELDS WAVE A GENTLE GOOD-BYE
AND TRY TO WHISPER TO YOUR SOUL
AS YOU WALK
TOWARD A DISTANT LINE
WHERE YOUR FUTURE WILL UNFOLD

Near Schmidt Beach

In summer, with friends,
you have good times
mostly by just letting them happen.

Early in the morning
the flat lake water
and still dark trees of Copper Island beckon.
Boats rev up; skiers gear up.
Out there the motor-induced wind
the flashy water
and the rising sun
will be your constant companions.

Back in the A-frame,
a clock high on the wall
crunches out the summer seconds
(if you really must keep track of time).
Instead, you could just lie there
relax
and listen to the familiar sounds
of a home
at breakfast time.

When you're ready
you might get up
sit on the deck
with coffee mug in hand
and contemplate this day
as it begins to gently unfold
in summer, with friends.

Flight

Hawk that sits on my gloved hand
listen closely—understand.
Hear my secret, desperate plea;
it has a sense of urgency.

Take me with you; take me now.
Perform some magic; (I don't know how).
We'll soar above the human throng
and head for the trees and sky beyond.

We'll glide above the pettiness,
over the greed and callousness.
The violence we'll leave below;
it won't affect us anymore.

From our new height, when we look down,
we will see a distant town,
where a golden river winds its way
through a quiet, placid, avian day.

An Encounter

I met a man named Courage
and he took me to his home;
I wanted so much to be like him
where ever I might roam.

He showed me glorious picture books
he kept by his fireside.
He told me of adventure
and the solitude of his ride.

For he said he often traveled alone;
the path was up to him.
And if I wanted his help at all,
I had to look within.

He quietly put his books away
and showed me to the door.
As I turned to wave good-bye,
I felt stronger than before.

I MET A MAN NAMED COURAGE
and he took me to his home
I wanted so much to be like him
where ever I might roam

He showed me glorious picture books
he kept by his fireside
He told me of adventure
and the solitude of his ride

For he said he often traveled alone
the path was up to him
And if I wanted his help at all
I had to look within

He quietly put his books away
And showed me to the door

AS I TURNED TO WAVE GOOD-BYE
I FELT STRONGER THAN BEFORE

Opening Act

Standing in front of this crowded room,
thumping heart and guitar in tune,
he mumbles a word or two about his song.
Though it's not him they're here to see,
they respond at first quite pleasantly,
giving him a sense that he belongs.

Yet to them, he's just some college kid;
they're not aware of the dreams in his head
and how he sings the secrets of his heart.
They soon get lost in their talk and beer,
moving chairs till a space is clear,
so serving girls can play their valued part.

He attacks the strings on his old guitar,
ignores the noise in this ancient bar
and plays the way he's practiced for so long.
For a hundred bucks and a beer in hand,
this gig is just a one night stand,
a time when he must keep his spirit strong.

Would he love to be the star of this night,
own the hits and play them just right,
and see the patrons hang on every word?
At this point in time it's hard to see
if that will ever become his reality;
he's got no reason yet to be self-assured.

He'll continue to sing to distracted crowds
that drink their booze and get too loud,
but he's hoping there will be a better time.
He knows he really has no choice;
the songs inside demand a voice
and he is just a servant of rhythm and rhyme.

Hemingway's Old Man

On the tourist beach at Varadero
I was thinking of the fisherman Santiago
and how those days and nights with that fish
were maybe the best ones of his life
because he was alone, suffering, enduring,
      and doing what he was born to do
      and dreaming of the lions too.

I understand how he loved that marlin,
yet caught and killed it.
Why wouldn't he love the fish
that ended his slump of eighty-four days?
It had been a burden so terrible
he was resigned to fish alone,
the boy ordered to a different boat.

There is no denying he broke his slump.
The sharks only stole what was already his
and we all know how that feels.

In the long run
he would be better off than those sharks
who had no sense of the contest
of the love
of the history.

Old man
sleep well on your bed of newspapers.
There will be more baseball games tomorrow;
more slumps will begin or continue or end
      and the lions may come to the shore
      and be with you once more.

Admiration

Oh to be ten, ass on your skateboard
cruising downhill in the middle of Royal Poinciana Drive.

With tee-shirt flapping and blond hair flipping,
you know damn well there's a car behind you.

Hey, that's not your worry;
you've done this a hundred times.

You glance over your shoulder,
board weaving, accelerating.

You apply the Fred Flintstone brakes,
manage the speed bumps,

lean into a hard right,
and snake toward the gravel shoulder.

A dusty, pebbly stop places you
beside your buddy.

As I rumble past in my two thousand pound machine,
I give you a thumbs up.

You just smile.
Me too.

My Neighbour's Patio

On summer Sunday afternoons, my next door neighbour,
bent over and shuffling during the rest of the week,
becomes animated as he prepares to host old pals and gals.

From our side of a white fence, my Mayday tree and I watch him,
all morning in the sunshine, sweeping and arranging,
until his backyard patio looks like a set for a stage play.

Soon an old record player atop an unsteady cart is rolled into place
and the annoyingly clear strings of Mantovani's orchestra
fill our gardens.

His guests do not arrive until my tree—
dark limbs and upper branches leaning over the fence—
casts a shadow across the patio.

Then, amidst an array of Tilley hats, oversized sunglasses, white arms,
white legs, and ridiculous white socks,
I can hear him brag about his patio's location
and the tree whose emerald leaves shade his cronies and him.

Martinis and wine fuel good-naturedness, especially in my neighbour,
who gives me an exaggerated wave from his darkened lawn chair
as though we are friends, as though we like each other.

You see, each October my neighbour actually speaks to me,
but only about the fallen leaves from "that damned tree"
and how they're everywhere: in his gutters, on his patio stones,
(and probably in his dreams).

"The tree's too big for your little yard," he complains.
"You've let it get out of hand."
What do I intend to do about it.
Will I at least clean up the damn leaves.

After a quiet consultation with my Mayday tree
and, might I add, with its blessing,
I pray that next summer there will be tree lashing winds
and thunderstorms on Sunday afternoons.

Lines

Lines on the mountains that glaciers carve
point to the heavens as beautiful scars.

Nature has her intrinsic way
of marking this Earth day after day.

But the lines we draw in the shifting sand
may not be a part of God's great plan.

Borders and battle lines keep us apart
and sap the strength of the human heart.

Lines to the left and lines to the right,
candidates arguing all through the night.

Side lines, base lines, centre lines too,
lines that separate the chosen few.

Those that divide lovers and friends,
a line at the start and a line at the end.

Lines we've created through jealousy
and her kindred spirit—secrecy.

Lines our lonely ones cut in their wrists,
love so frail, they cannot resist.

Lines we've sworn we wouldn't cross;
now they remind us of what we have lost.

Borders and battle lines keep us apart
and sap the strength of the human heart

Breathing in School

Turning Points

Just when I thought I wasn't going to be able to handle September,
you smiled and said, "Good to see you back; did you miss me?"
And I was okay again.

Just when I thought I couldn't mark another paper,
you wrote something very important
and I kept on reading.

Just when I was at a point of frustration,
you looked concerned and said, "Take it easy."
And so I did, or at least tried to.

Just when I thought I might lower my expectations,
you showed me what you were really capable of doing
and I asked for more.

Just when I finally realized how much I appreciate your talents,
you quietly told me, "It's June; I need to leave now."
And I waved good-bye.

Stress

All the other wide-eyed grade one children
in our walking-together-the-first-week group
had their information letters signed by a parent or guardian.

All these scrubbed-behind-the ears neophytes
would proudly and dutifully present them
to the new most influential lady in their little worlds
when they were called upon (in alphabetical order, of course)
to bring them to the big desk at the front of their polished classroom,
all the children, except me.

And there would be, as promised, a gold star placed beside
each of their incredibly neat, hand-printed names
 on a wall chart with perfectly measured columns
 (enough for weeks and weeks of achievements),
shiny stars for all the children, except me.

Such a discovery, on a September morning where the sun,
though weakening already after Canadian Labour Day,
was glaring in my freckled face.
Yes, as we herded together near a busy intersection,
all but one of us had clutched in our little hands
the required document, expected back today,
the first real test of our intelligence,
of our readiness to face the solemn responsibilities
of first grade students at Tuxedo Park Elementary.

I turned and ran
back along the familiar sidewalk
that accepted each of my tiny strides without forgiveness.
I accelerated past Tommy Hannam's house and Eddie Anderson's too.
I switched on an ambulance siren wail.
Mrs. Kennedy, mother of Jimmy my best friend (who had his letter),
was shaking a rug on her front steps,
dust caught in the summer sun like smoke from a campfire.
"Keithie, what's the matter?"
No words could encapsulate this emergency; I howled louder.
Tears blurred my windshield.

I cut across Gow's front yard, noticing only that their house guest
was lounging next to his shiny convertible, staring at me.
"Mommy!" erupted from inside a scream.
 She was there; her beautiful face behind the screen of our front door.
"My letter, my letter!"
She turned away; came back moments later.
She had it—signed!
As simple as that.
Then the sudden realization I would now be late for school,
six blocks away.
We had no car.
A fresh crop of tears, a higher pitched calamity.

Gow's house guest rescues us.
His gleaming machine luxuriously transports us to school in no time,
Mom's arm cozied around her tear-stained first grader,
his chest rising, falling, shuddering,
siren turned off.

We arrive as the children are shuffling into single file lines,
the old brick building ready to embrace them.
"I have my letter too," I imagine announcing,
but who among them should care?

Inside teachers' desks, there are boxes of gold stars,
(blue, red, and silver too),
ready to be licked and thumb placed
beside precisely printed names of deserving boys and girls.

Queen of the Junior High

Oh yes! Oh yes!
She has arrived.
God save the ninth grade Queen of Junior High.

Well before the late bell rings,
her entourage strolls the crowded hall
like royalty arriving at the ball.

To whom will she speak
on this gossipy day?
Should her subjects step forward or stay out of her way?

Boys, like court jesters,
vie for her attention,
crowd in close, hope to be mentioned.

At a distance,
even teachers stand in awe.
Yet some of them can see the flaws.

They wonder what will be next for her—
abdication or graduation?

oh yes!
oh yes!
SHE HAS ARRIVED
God save the ninth grade
Queen
of junior high

Drop Out

Adolescent cave man
sits outside the school.
His boom box fire
keeps him cool.

Hair down to his shoulders
leather jacket on his back,
must have been a time warp
that knocked him off the track.

He used to be on the inside
trying to make the grade.
Now he's looking Neanderthal
in his classroom in the shade.

On Changing Schools

There was a time when I thought that I
could stay right here forever,
but "all things must pass" and maybe that's
not for the worse, but for the better.

Time moves on; outlooks change;
people come and go.
Given all we've been through, I'll remember you.
That's something you should know.

Jeremy

What a little life I would have lived.
What a little world I would have seen,
if I, like you, had died
at seventeen.

What a lot of love I would have missed.
What a pile of shattered dreams,
if I, like you, were made to wonder
what might have been.

No Way Out

I am a prisoner of a war
waged inside and outside my mind.

Who is the enemy that surrounds me?

All day, barbed wire voices
enclose me, confine me.

Machine-gunned questions, suspicious looks—
How will I escape the dangerous barrage
of commands and sarcasm?

If only I had the means to counter-attack
 or flee.

But no—
I am a junior high student;
I am a prisoner of war.

Poem for Smarter Poets than Me

If only I could dive as deeply as you
into that dark ocean of observations, reflections, and discoveries,
without being taken aback by murky phrases
that probably aren't murky at all.

If only I could read with your confident poet's voice
and avoid the distraction of vocabulary and allusions
that lie just beyond my grasp.
Should I know of Plath? Sorry.

The ideas are there,
buried treasure on the fault line,
but sharks are lurking,
their academic eyes noncommittal,
and the key for the chest dangles from another's neck.

If I could dive as deeply as you,
I wouldn't drown.

If I could
dive as deeply
as you
I wouldn't
drown

Poetry Lesson

"Let's think about the higher level."

Now, what the hell is that?
A hot dog in the upper deck
far from ball and bat?

Your "higher level" don't touch my soul;
it's talk that's over my head.
It's based on some obscure ideas
in dusty books you've read.

Keep it to yourself; don't lay it on me;
there's a ball game on tonight:
peanuts, beer, my mind at rest
beneath the stadium lights.

Peanuts, beer, my mind at rest
beneath the stadium lights.

LET'S THINK ABOUT THE HIGHER LEVEL

Now what the hell is That?

Teacher to a Former Student

At the very least
you could have left me a lesson plan, David,
before you killed yourself.

What was I supposed to do with your classmates today?
They knew.
I knew.
What was I supposed to do:

> Read them an inadequate poem?
> Carry on as usual?
> What?

We were so quiet.
Words did not come easily.
We looked at each other
as though we were the guilty ones.
We should have known, right?

But yesterday
you were the class clown
as usual.
You couldn't sit still
as usual.
I almost kept you after class
as usual.

I should have, David;
we should have talked.

Before you went home
and took your father's gun
and went to his bedroom
we should have talked.

Dancing at the Junior High

Girls too tall
Guys too short
Shoes too tight
But it's a start
All dressed up
Feelings inside
Huddle in the middle
A place to hide
Dancing at the junior high

Watching pop stars
On a video screen
Making night moves
They've never seen
Given a chance
They think they might
But everyone knows
It won't happen tonight
Dancing at the junior high

Sooner and later
Tears in the eyes
Somebody's hurt
Somebody cries
Some things get said
Some things don't
He wishes he could
She knows he won't
Dancing at the junior high

The music stops
The evening ends
He thinks of her
And she of him
Each head home
A little more blue
Regret lives on
When they're through
Dancing at the junior high

Grade Nines in June

You're getting ready to leave, aren't you?
I can see it in your eyes,
hear it in your silence,
feel it when you sigh.

Don't worry;
it's okay.
You're eager for something new.
But when you look back at junior high
say, "I learned; I grew."

Breathing in the Dark

Crow and Cat

Somewhat embarrassed and self-conscious
about his discovery,
a huge crow stands beside a dead cat
lying softly against a curb
on Memorial Drive.

At a nearby traffic light,
morning rush hour cars
roar and stop and wait
and roar again.

Our shiny automobiles
and the bright October sun
seem out of place at this somber scene.

The crow glances at us,
wishing we would go away,
so he could privately enjoy his gruesome prize.

The Secret

Like titles of movies
That won't appear on your bill
The secret is yours
Your lips are still

It's below the surface
Below the lies
Below the places
You usually hide

It's behind the dreams
Behind the laughter
Behind this life
And what comes after

It's inside your heart
Inside your mind
Beside darkest wishes
Of a different kind

Won't you face the music
Let it out in the open
Speak the words
That have remained unspoken

Confess to the crime
You're not alone
Even your judges
Commit sins of their own

But like titles of movies
That won't appear on your bill
The secret is yours
And your lips are still

Confess to the crime
You're not alone
Even your judges
Commit Sins of their own

Robber

You stole my thoughts
and wrote them down.
You photocopied
my constant frown.

You tape recorded
the beat of my heart.
You auditioned well
and got my part.

You photographed
my darkest soul.
Then buried it alive
 in an unmarked hole.

When all was done
and you'd had my say,
you simply told me
to go away.

you photographed
my darkest soul
then buried it
alive ROBBER
in an
unmarked
hole

Late Night News

The media love bad news.
Death and suffering excite them.
Misery and heartbreak grab their attention,
make them slither closer,
   electric cables hissing
   electric eyes staring
   electric ears leaning in:

a dismembered body in a farmer's field
   a son
   or a daughter
somber police at a news conference
   no suspects, no suspects, no suspects.

Close up on a child's photo.
Zoom in on a mother's trembling hands.
Interview the family
 sadness personified.

Show us the worst of mankind;
dwell on it.
Fold back a white sheet from the corpse of human dignity.

Take us to places we don't want to go;
entice us to look. (Then, we wish we hadn't.)

Say good night;
send us to darkened beds
where our nightmares try to make sense of it all.

fold
back
a white
sheet
from the corpse of
human dignity

Where Do They Sleep?

Under the neon glow of the Las Vegas Strip,
little Latino men and women smack their ridiculous hooker cards
and flick them toward mainly disinterested sightseers and revelers.

They stand restless, perhaps embarrassed,
on the edges of public sidewalks
in front of some of the grandest hotels in North America.

Smack and flick.

Can you hear them hours later, as you momentarily lift your head
from your fresh pillow on Bellagio's twentieth floor?

Do you wonder what they think of this work
where dignity takes a back seat to an empty belly and a crying child?

And in what dark corner of Las Vegas
do they lay down their weary bones
and let their heads drop against rumpled jackets?

Never mind.
It's all understood.
They have their cards to peddle
and you have your disdain.

Instructions

Let the cold seep under your door
Let it creep across your floor
Let it seize your heart and soul
Let it exact its awful toll

Allow it to freeze your burning desires
Suffer it to smother the hopeful fires
Then ice can bury your fantasy
And the killing frost may set you free

Dangerous Poems

I like dangerous poems.
When you get too close,
they burn you
or cause your heart to miss a beat.

I like poems that take you to the edge,
throw you over, and then save you,
just before you hit rock bottom.

I like poems that put into words
crimes you know you have committed,
but won't confess to.
I like dangerous poems.

WHEN
YOU
GET
TOO
CLOSE
they
burn
you
OR CAUSE
YOUR
HEART
TO
MISS
A
BEAT

After All This
(September, 2001)

When will America smile again
When will we see her laugh
When will the standup comics
Be able to get on track

How can we laugh aloud again
When the worst of human kind
Has altered the lives of everyone
With hate that is so blind

Will we find the human strength
To rebuild our wounded faith
So we can come together
To share this precious space

From a Distance

There were heroes on September eleventh,
but I do not know their names.
There were heroes on that dreadful day
amidst the smoke and flames.

Tuesday morning heroes
who did the best they could
on battlefields so bizarre
no one understood.

I think about them often,
but I can't bear to watch them die
over and over and over again
through the media's callous eye.

View Point

I took a turn for the worse and parked it,
shut off the engine, but left the radio on.

I didn't know whether to get out of the car
or just sit there and peer over the dashboard.

Across the valley, the city looked as quiet
and beautiful as an empty movie set.

Maybe everyone had left.

Wouldn't that be funny?

I had driven up here on this dark, dead-end road
to get away from them and they had already gone,

maybe to get away from me.

On a City Bus

Inside a downtown bus amid an electric glare,
pawns of the business world vacantly stare.

Monetary stress from the market place
hangs upon every Dow Jones face.

The bus roars on, hauling them away
from their IBM's and an empty feeling day.

Tomorrow promises more of the same,
a Xerox copy of this city life game.

Consolidation

I'm in cleanup mode.
Somewhere, I need to find a cardboard box:
television size, maybe refrigerator size.

Into it I will place—
no, I will dump—
emotions that weigh a ton,
have sharp edges, and take up too much space.

I'm talking about all the stuff the world elicits from me:
    despair
       regret
          loss
              helplessness
                  indignation
                      frustration
                        anger
                            embarrassment
                              humiliation
                              guilt.

Then, I'll phone Fed-Ex or UPS,
whoever can get here fastest.

By the time they arrive,
pushing a dolly with oversized wheels,
I will have emptied the packing tape dispenser.

By God, whoever tries to open this
will have their work cut out for them.

And the annoying details about sender and receiver—
I'll lie about everything.

Finally, I'll label it
with a big, black indelible marker:
    SADNESS

Just Breathing

Armstrong's Discovery

What if—
when Neil walked on the moon
he had found
a stainless steel dinner spoon?

Would that have been enough
to make mankind swoon?

And would we,
in our intellect, make room
for a singular, sandy, lunar spoon?

Poem Search

I am searching through a book
that contains fine poetry by respected poets.
I am looking for a piece I love,
but have forgotten to bookmark.

When I find it, this elusive poem will
    speak to me
    comfort me
    scrape my heart
    make me remember.

I search and search the pages;
fine words and elegant phrases flash by
like the lighted windows of a passenger train.

Maybe I'm mistaken.
    Perhaps the poem is elsewhere.
    Maybe it hasn't even been written yet.
    Maybe I'm the one who has to write it.

Skies

From my tiny backyard in the city,
I stare at a strip of sky.
And it seems to stare right back at me
like a pale blue alien eye.

But when I'm far from the city,
the sky is soft and wide.
It has the look of a country friend,
of one who will stay close by.

Political Man

Hey, little, little political man,
you mainly just want to shake my hand
or hold a baby and cuddle him close—
photo opportunities mean the most.

You wear a conservative, pin-striped suit
no matter what your political roots,
and those brand new, polished platform shoes
might determine whether you win or lose.
Yet the closer we get to Election Day,
it's your too white smile that's in my way.

All the truths that people seek
get very muddled when you speak.
Sometimes you sound slightly left of middle;
when you shift to the right, it's all a riddle.
You trot out promises you can't keep
and chant party slogans in your sleep.
At the end of your long political day,
do you really care what I have to say?

Hey, little, little political man
trying to lead us to the Promised Land,
after the House, you can sit in the Senate:
such a career, such a place to end it.

Blairmore – Coleman

This is workplace Alberta.
The mountains lean in like foremen
waiting for you to do something.

No time for the new age coffee shop
on weekday mornings.

Best to grab a Styrofoam version
up at the gas station on the highway
stir it while you clump back to the truck
your head down
twenty things to do at the jobsite before lunch
rattling through your mind
aided and abetted by the Crowsnest wind.

In a Mexican Square

A tourist mom takes her young son
to a Mexican village square;
a bit of local culture
she hopes to show him there.

They'll spend an hour or two away
from their all-inclusive resort,
its all you can eat buffet
and its beachside rental sports.

With the sun and birds as companions,
they sit in a quiet space
and watch the local residents
stroll through this gentle place.

Soon an old native woman
in tattered, colourful array
limps into the sun-washed square
and sits down across the way.

A wide-brimmed hat and senior's shades
darken most of her wrinkled face,
while skirts of mauve and pink and green
make her far from commonplace.

With a shopping sack across her arm
and a shawl that sadly sags,
she reaches deep inside its folds
and finds a paper bag.

From it, she scatters popcorn,
as though in a chicken pen,
but it's pigeons she attracts,
more and more of them.

They bob their iridescent heads
as if they're in a trance
and edge a little nearer
to such benevolence.

Bending a little closer,
not just to spread the wealth,
she grabs a bird in a heartbeat
with measured, practiced stealth.

She wrings its neck in a moment
and thrusts it in the sack,
then shuffles slowly from the square,
the sun upon her back.

Alarmed, the boy looks at his mom,
she whispers to him, "And so,
now you've had a first hand look
at a different Mexico."

Foreign Territory

I got my passport stamped by a man
who looked slightly military.
Now that, I could understand.

But what I didn't need
was the way he winked at me
as he leaned close and touched my hand.

Breakaway

I wish I could slow it all down like in a movie.
I imagine that's what Bobby and Wayne and Mario can do.
Everyone else is bustin' his ass,
but it's all syrupy slow to them.

What I really needed to do, you see,
was fake the snap shot
freeze the goalie
maybe even freeze the mook that was behind me,
then gather the puck back in
like a delicate black bird
start to pull it over to my backhand
get Black Pads movin' to his left a little
and then with my Sherwood wand
drag it to my forehand left
as I lean and glide to the right.

Can you picture it?
Now I've got that stick side corner open.
I just need to slide it in there;
right along the ice'll be fine.

Life Span

Nothing is as brown
as the bottom of a puddle.
Nothing.

I have one expanding beside
the austere concrete of my driveway.
Each July thunderstorm contributes generously
to its brown-bottomed growth.

Yesterday, during a sun break,
I saw bubbles rising within this translucent world,
breaking the surface
and rippling away in concentric circles.

It was as if mysterious creatures
lived below the cracked puddle floor
and their breathing exposed their hiding place.

How ridiculous; it's only a puddle.
What creatures could prosper
in such a tentative world?

It was as if
mysterious creatures
lived beneath
the cracked puddle floor
and their breathing
exposed their hiding place

"If we were all [put] on trial for our thoughts, we would all be hanged."
–Margaret Atwood, *Alias Grace*

Getting Published

The committee members, eight of them,
were seated at a long table facing me.
They were dressed in dark suits,
identical in the somber lighting.
"Mr. Worthington," the chairman began,
"we've decided to publish all of your thoughts."

"You what?"

"Yes, that's right.
The committee has met and deliberated.
We're confident of an audience.
We have them all here you know. On disk."
He patted a plastic container on the table.
"Up to date as of last night.
We don't offer remuneration,
but we thought it courteous to let you know.
You might want to make plans."

"Plans?"

"Yes. You understand that not everyone
will be pleased with all of your thoughts."

I stared at the container
just beyond arm's reach,
imagining it suddenly destroyed.

"We have back-up copies,
multiple copies," emphasized the chairman.

"I see."

"Good luck, Mr. Worthington. And good-bye."